BLUES
BUSTERS

Suggestions for Beating the Blues

Blues Busters
Suggestions for Beating the Blues

By

Jessica Paige   Michele Paige

● BLUES BUSTERS ●

Cover photo: Photodisc, Inc.

To contact the authors or to order additional copies:

Turtle Press
401 Silas Deane Hwy
PO Box 290206
Wethersfield CT 06129-0206
1-800-778-8785

ISBN 1-880336-10-3

● BLUES BUSTERS ●

Introduction

When the mailman handed us our mail, we immediately knew it was bad news; after all, good news rarely arrives in a skinny envelope. Sure enough, we had been rejected . . . from the circus. After weeks of learning to juggle and attempting to master the unicycle, that fateful letter dashed our hopes of attending Clown College and becoming Ringling Bros. & Barnum and Bailey clowns. When we look back on it now, it all seems a bit crazy, but at the time we had an acute case of the blues.

Our sad mood just seemed to feed upon itself - until one of us remembered a bag of gourmet jelly beans saved for just such an occasion. As we sat there eating Root Beer and Pina Colada beans, things seemed more cheerful. We started joking that we couldn't even run away and join the circus! If we hadn't remembered our cache of jelly beans, I doubt we would have been laughing so hard - if at all. When the blues strike, most people mope around fixating on their sadness allowing it to spiral out of control. Thus, in between

● BLUES BUSTERS ●

munches, we resolved to break the spiral and make something positive out of our rejection: we would plant a tree, so to speak. Although our rejection for the circus forced us to hang up our big red noses and our size 16 shoes, it planted the seeds of *Blues Busters*.

Everybody experiences the blues now and again, but not everyone knows their equivalent of a bag of jelly beans. As you read through these blues busters, circle or highlight those which you think would make you happy when blue. In this way you will be prepared to deal with life's inevitable transient sad times. Of course if the sadness is more serious, professional help might be needed. We hope that you and your friends enjoy reading *Blues Busters* as much as we enjoyed writing it.

Best of Luck and Keep Smiling!

● BLUES BUSTERS ●

Dear Readers,

If you would like to share some of your suggestions for beating the blues, please write to us. Our address is:

Blues Busters
c/o Turtle Press
PO Box 290206
Wethersfield CT 06129-0206

● BLUES BUSTERS ●

1. Eat gourmet jelly beans. ☺

2. Sit on the beach and gaze
   at the sun as it falls
   below the horizon. ☺

3. Take a strawberry jello bath.☺

4. Shower with your pet parrot. ☺

5. Dance to some oldies on top
of your desk. ☺

6. Take a hot shower until your
fingers prune. ☺

7. Get your hair cut or just experiment
with a new hair style. ☺

8. Buy a new outfit. ☺

9. Plant a tree (figuratively and literally). ☺

10. Take a catnap with your cat. ☺

11. Buy a Rolodex and organize
your life for greater efficiency. ☺

● BLUES BUSTERS ●

12. Call your mother. ☺

13. Don't call your mother. ☺

14. Attend a play, concert, or vaudeville show. ☺

15. Have a thick, rich milk shake or gooey sundae. ☺

16. Bungee jump. ☺

17. Visit the aquarium and feed the fish. ☺

18. Sit in the sun and let the rays touch your face. ☺

19. Take a walk in the park and feed the pigeons. ☺

20. Attend the taping of a television talk show or sitcom. ☺

21. Play a game of pick-up basketball. ☺

22. Go for a massage and bring your own scented lotion or oil. ☺

23. Relax in a jacuzzi. ☺

24. Take a beggar to lunch. ☺

25. Watch toddlers playing in the park. ☺

26. Paint a picture of the most
beautiful place on Earth. ☺

27. Go to the gym and exercise until your body feels like jello. ☺

28. Watch a romantic move like Casablanca, Gone with the Wind, or Like Water for Chocolate.☺

29. Make a kite and fly it. ☺

30. Talk to yourself
- you might just get some answers. ☺

31. Brew a love potion made of rose petals,
thyme, and camomile. ☺

32. Go for a NASCAR driving lesson. ☺

33. Focus and refocus on your short-term and long-term goals. ☺

34. Make your own homemade bubble gum. ☺

35. Get front row seats at a ball game. ☺

36. Thoroughly clean the house.☺

37. Join a neighborhood team sport. ☺

38. Make a list of all the things about yourself that make your proud. ☺

39. Take a hike through the woods. ☺

40. Go horse-back riding. ☺

41. Take a day-long cruise. ☺

42. Dream about the perfect future. ☺

43. Wear your sexiest underwear. ☺

44. Treat yourself to dinner at the most expensive restaurant you know. ☺

45. Play the piano (with your toes). ☺

46. Experiment a little and do something crazy - something no one would expect you to do. ☺

47. Brew your own homemade beer. ☺

48. Check into a bed and breakfast
for the day. ☺

49. Start a new collection. ☺

**50. Say "I love you"
to someone you love.** ☺

51. Volunteer your time to a charity. ☺

52. Make a gift for someone special. ☺

53. Play ball with a child. ☺

54. Wash your car until it shines. ☺

55. Bird watch at a national park. ☺

56. Throw an evening tea party. ☺

57. Nibble on your lover's ear. ☺

58. Watch "It's a Wonderful Life" again and again and again. ☺

59. Buy a sheet cake and decorate it with candy and frosting. ☺

60. Reminisce with the help of family photo albums; think of a funny story for each photo. ☺

BLUES BUSTERS

61. Try a new exotic Vietnamese dish. ☺

62. Buy yourself a bouquet of
freeze dried flowers. ☺

63. Get a new part-time job in an
industry that has always fascinated you. ☺

64. Eat at a greasy spoon and forget about cholesterol, fat, and calories. ☺

65. Speak to your priest, rabbi, or minister about your problems. ☺

66. Read this book. ☺

67. Listen to nature sounds music while showering or bathing in the dark. ☺

68. Randomly call an international phone number and talk to whomever answers. ☺

69. Write a letter to a pen pal. ☺

70. Raid the refrigerator in the middle of the night. ☺

71. Go to an open house. ☺

72. Go to a fireman's carnival. ☺

73. Attend church services. ☺

74. Just hold hands with your lover. ☺

75. Have a cook-out at the beach. ☺

76. Paint your bedroom a cheerful shade of yellow. ☺

77. Clean out your closet and throw out things you haven't used in years and will never use. ☺

78. Take a Latin dance class. ☺

79. Ride the biggest roller coaster at your favorite theme park. ☺

80. Learn a new magic trick
and try it out on your friends. ☺

81. Call your long time crush. ☺

82. Crash a party at your alma mater. ☺

83. Rent a limo for the night and go on an evening tour of the city. ☺

84. Go to the races and place a bet on the long shot. ☺

85. Take out an atlas and pick out places you would like to visit. ☺

86. Take part in a community production of a play. ☺

87. Treat yourself to a new handbag. ☺

88. Throw your name in for a local election. ☺

89. Call your Chamber of Commerce for suggestions on local tourist attractions you can visit. ☺

90. Weed your garden. ☺

91. Change your name for a day or go by a new nickname. ☺

92. Cook a new dish. ☺

93. Give to the poor. ☺

94. Produce a show for Public Access. ☺

95. Take in a stray cat. ☺

96. Take a nap outside in a hammock. ☺

97. Visit a country store and
buy homemade crafts. ☺

98. Play a game of Laser Tag
in the basement. ☺

99. Write a poem in iambic pentameter for someone you love. ☺

100. Sing in the rain. ☺

101. Buy a piece of funky costume jewelry. ☺

102. Watch a parade. ☺

103. Start a conversation with
a complete stranger. ☺

104. Cook your favorite childhood dish. ☺

105. Write down your strengths and successes. ☺

106. Read a scary mystery in bed. ☺

107. Give yourself a foot massage. ☺

108. Put your name on the
Mercedes Convertible waiting list. ☺

109. Buy yourself a new hat. ☺

110. Write down all your problems
then toss the list in the fire
or flush it down the toilet. ☺

111. Burn some sandalwood incense. ☺

112. Take a hot bath by candlelight while sipping a glass of Chardonnay. ☺

113. Get your teeth cleaned at the dentist. ☺

114. Sit by a roaring fire toasting marshmallows and roasting chestnuts. ☺

115. Think how much worse your situation could be. ☺

116. Adopt a retired greyhound. ☺

117. Bring thirty dollars to the casino and play a couple of rounds of blackjack. ☺

118. Sit under a waterfall. ☺

119. Paint each fingernail a different color. ☺

120. Scream on the top of your lungs. ☺

121. Confront your problems. ☺

122. Buy a lottery ticket and play your lucky numbers. ☺

123. Hang out with your friends. ☺

124. Call or write to a friend whom you have not talked to in years. ☺

125. Make something for your home by following the instructions in a home magazine. ☺

BLUES BUSTERS ●

126. Meditate. ☺

127. Meditate nude. ☺

128. Draw a red smiley face on each hand to remind yourself to be happy. ☺

129. Swing on a swing. ☺

130. Go to the department store
and test smell all the
colognes and perfumes. ☺

131. Take a horse and carriage ride. ☺

132. Sleep over someone else's house. ☺

133. Jump up and down on your bed. ☺

134. Cook a favorite dish
for someone special. ☺

135. Try on all the sexy outfits
in your closet. ☺

136. Put a funny message on your answering machine. ☺

137. Tense all of your muscles and then relax them, one at a time. ☺

138. Share a personal secret with a loved one. ☺

139. Play footsies under the table. ☺

140. Eat your favorite foods,
but don't overindulge. ☺

141. Make a card for someone special. ☺

142. Garden naked by moonlight. ☺

143. Read old comics from your childhood. ☺

144. Go to the library and read books to children. ☺

145. Do sit-ups until your abs burn like hell. ☺

146. Jump rope in the rain. ☺

147. Design your own costume jewelry. ☺

148. Travel to an exotic destination like Tahiti. ☺

149. Buy a water bed. ☺

150. Call a help line. ☺

151. Curl, straighten or crimp your hair. ☺

152. Sip some chamomile tea. ☺

153. Order Chinese take-out. ☺

154. Answer a personal ad. ☺

155. Draw caricatures of people
on the city bus. ☺

156. Buy a funky new pair of shoes. ☺

157. Think back to a good
childhood memory. ☺

158. Recycle and heal Mother Earth. ☺

159. Watch Sesame Street. ☺

160. Skip. ☺

161. Start a model kit. ☺

162. Take an art class at a local studio. ☺

163. Start a patchwork quilt. ☺

164. Wear satin pajamas and slip in between satin sheets. ☺

165. Redecorate your room. ☺

166. Subscribe to a new magazine. ☺

167. Treat yourself and your
lover to breakfast in bed. ☺

168. Buy yourself a dozen helium balloons. ☺

169. Read an inspirational poem. ☺

170. Take a self-proclaimed holiday. ☺

171. Visit a Christmas decorations store. ☺

172. Walk your dog or someone else's. ☺

173. Sing Christmas carols. ☺

174. Try out for the circus. ☺

175. Smell the roses. ☺

176. Find new and interesting ways to be passionate with your lover. ☺

177. Start on a project you have been meaning to do for a long time. ☺

178. Make homemade ice cream. ☺

179. Go bowling. ☺

180. Look through your old
high school yearbook. ☺

181. Read the biography of a famous person you admire. ☺

182. Take a mud bath. ☺

183. Visit an art gallery. ☺

184. Sing the hymns in church. ☺

185. Listen to some soothing music you haven't listened to in years. ☺

186. Attend an educational lecture. ☺

187. Feed your lover without utensils. ☺

188. Buy a piece of fancy electronic equipment. ☺

189. Have a wine and cheese tasting party. ☺

190. Go shopping in a chichi part of town. ☺

191. Play co-ed naked Twister. ☺

192. Experiment with aromatherapy. ☺

193. Take in the smells of a gourmet deli. ☺

194. Write a love letter to yourself and mail it. ☺

195. Watch a comedy show. ☺

196. Soak your feet in hot water. ☺

197. Browse through a toy store
and treat yourself to a toy
you always wanted
but never had as a child. ☺

198. Count your blessings - literally. ☺

199. Watch Saturday morning cartoons. ☺

200. Plan a romantic adventure for two. ☺

201. Reminisce about some of the best times of your life. Assure yourself that there will be many more. ☺

202. Sit cross-legged on a high pile rug and make paper angel cut-outs. ☺

203. Watch an old television show you haven't seen since elementary school. ☺

204. Get a good night's sleep. ☺

205. Watch television in bed. ☺

206. Take a shower in the dark. ☺

207. Dance under the moon and stars. ☺

208. Go frog and salamander hunting. ☺

209. Reorganize your files. ☺

210. Press flowers in a book. ☺

211. Take a midnight skinny dip
in a heated outdoor pool. ☺

212. Hire a strip-o-gram or
a sing-o-gram for yourself. ☺

213. Melt chocolate and
reform it in funny shapes. ☺

214. Karaoke all night. ☺

215. Play freeze tag in the sprinkler. ☺

216. Build a snowman. ☺

217. Donate blood. ☺

218. Let your hair down and vigorously massage your scalp. ☺

219. Rent and watch all the movie classics you've never seen. ☺

220. Pet a puppy in a pet shop. ☺

221. Get that expensive sexy little slip dress that you've been eyeing for weeks but were too chicken to buy. ☺

222. Buy CDs of your old favorites. ☺

223. Buy a new book. ☺

224. Tease your hair to the ceiling. ☺

225. Volunteer to teach Sunday school. ☺

226. Go sledding down a steep hill. ☺

227. Crochet or needlepoint. ☺

228. Gaze at the city skyline at night. ☺

229. Go to a casino and catch a show and a buffet. ☺

230. Go incognito. ☺

231. Visit New Orleans for Mardi-Gras. ☺

232. Visit a relative or friend you
haven't seen in a while;
your thoughtfulness will cheer them. ☺

233. Buy postcards of your hometown
and send them to friends. ☺

234. When the phone rings pick it up and say, "Hi, may I speak to Susan?" ☺

235. Visit Disneyland. ☺

236. Have your ears pierced. ☺

237. Kidnap your lover for a romantic evening on the town or at home. ☺

238. Take goofy Polaroids of yourself. ☺

239. Enter a beauty contest. ☺

240. Read "The Far Side." ☺

241. Play miniature golf. ☺

242. Do a kind deed for a stranger. ☺

243. Take a drive in the country. ☺

244. Discover how many people can fit in a phone booth. ☺

245. Vacation on a tropical island. ☺

246. People-watch at the mall. ☺

247. Sift through the stuff in your attic. ☺

248. Do a crossword or jigsaw puzzle. ☺

249. Snuggle under the covers with
your significant other. ☺

250. Research something you've been meaning to know the answer to for years. ☺

251. Throw a penny in a fountain and make a wish. ☺

252. Look back at how far you've come.☺

253. Start your diet. ☺

254. Break your diet. ☺

255. Send an anonymous love
note and a rose to someone
you have a crush on. ☺

256. Clear your mind and
relax on the floor. ☺

257. Do some mundane tasks
(e.g. reorganize your telephone
or address book). ☺

258. Hunt for bargains at a yard sale. ☺

259. Sit in a meadow under a tree. ☺

260. Go mountain climbing. ☺

261. Chat with friends on the Internet. ☺

262. Get lost in a crowd. ☺

263. Volunteer to work with
disabled children. ☺

264. Read while taking a bath. ☺

265. Set new goals
and vow to reach them. ☺

266. See what's happening at your
local civic center:
Rodeos
Professional wrestling
Ice skating extravaganzas
Monster truck shows
Home/Garden Fairs ☺

267. Sit on the floor while taking a shower. ☺

268. Write a thank you letter to someone who helped you recently. ☺

269. Dip your feet in a fountain. ☺

270. Wear an outfit you haven't worn in years but has great sentimental value to you. ☺

271. Visit a historical museum or restored village. ☺

272. Reread your old love
letters and poems. ☺

273. Sun yourself on the beach,
but remember to wear sunblock. ☺

274. Draw a picture of your pet. ☺

275. Find patterns, faces, and scenes in the shapes of clouds. ☺

276. Pot an evergreen. ☺

277. Watch the ice skaters at Rockefeller Center during the holidays. ☺

278. Visit a place where you have fond memories. ☺

279. Eat healthy; have a fruit salad, yogurt, or a tuna sandwich. ☺

280. Take a day off from your problems. ☺

281. Rent a Lamborghini for a day's spin. ☺

282. Frolic in the autumn wind. ☺

283. Strike up a conversation with a stranger. ☺

284. Bury the hatchet. ☺

285. Water your lawn. ☺

286. Have a picnic in front of a toasty fireplace. ☺

287. Give a loved one a present for no particular reason. ☺

288. Savor a cappuccino topped
with whipped cream at
an outdoor cafe. ☺

289. Slip your loved one a love note. ☺

290. Walk along the boardwalk. ☺

291. Go to a county fair and try your hand at winning a stuffed animal. ☺

292. Go to the airport and watch the airplanes take off. ☺

293. Play a game of midnight football with your friends. ☺

294. Visit the ocean and breathe in the fresh salt air. ☺

295. Have a marathon movie day. ☺

296. Visit a working farm and milk the cows, sheer the sheep, pet the baby animals and roll in the hay. ☺

297. Visit an arboretum. ☺

298. Take a deep breath.
Then take another. ☺

299. Sketch nature scenes. ☺

300. Stargaze. ☺

301. Pick wild berries and make berry pies. ☺

302. Give someone a compliment;
you'll be surprised at how good
it makes both of you feel. ☺

303. Visit your old neighborhood. ☺

304. Sing the Love Boat theme song. ☺

305. Swim in the moonlight. ☺

306. Sip hot cocoa in front of
a crackling fire. ☺

307. Wrap gifts. ☺

308. Buy on impulse. ☺

309. Go to a midnight car wash. ☺

310. Say, "What the hell!" and mean it. ☺

311. Have a barbecue even if it's winter. ☺

312. Just be goofy. ☺

313. Buy and collect gizmos. ☺

314. Sculpt a snow or sand dragon. ☺

315. Rub perfume and sweet scented body lotions all over yourself and your significant other. ☺

316. Collect autumn leaves and preserve them by placing them between two sheets of waxed paper and ironing. ☺

317. Take the phone off the hook. ☺

318. Jettison someone or something
that has been a source of
vexation in your life. ☺

319. Buy something outrageously
frivolous.☺

320. Doodle, doodle, doodle. ☺

321. Reminisce about good times in the company of friends. ☺

322. Volunteer to help school children learn how to read. ☺

323. Take time out to daydream. ☺

324. Browse through a used bookstore. ☺

325. Change your normal routines. ☺

326. Tie-dye your favorite t-shirt. ☺

327. Attend a fashion show. ☺

328. Exchange hopes and dreams
with a friend. ☺

BLUES BUSTERS

329. Go to a midnight ball game. ☺

330. Run through knee-high grass. ☺

331. Go bargain hunting at a thrift store. ☺

332. Go camping in your backyard. ☺

333. Take snapshots of breathtaking nature scenes. ☺

334. Watch an erotic film by yourself or with your significant other. ☺

335. Get on a bus and ride it all the way to the last stop. ☺

336. Arrange a secret romantic rendezvous with your lover. ☺

337. Smile at a stranger. ☺

338. Take a walk through the cemetery.
It just might put all your troubles
in perspective. ☺

339. Learn a new hobby such as origami,
stained glass window making
or sand patterning with a friend. ☺

340. Browse through a museum shop. ☺

341. Simmer herbs, letting the exotic
and pungent aroma waft
throughout the house. ☺

342. Plan a surprise birthday party. ☺

343. Make doll house furniture with whatever you find around the house. ☺

344. Warm yourself by a pot-bellied stove. ☺

345. Telephone a friend or loved one overseas. ☺

346. Start a scrapbook full of dried pressed flowers, fabric swatches, and old letters. ☺

347. Send a fan letter to your favorite movie star. ☺

348. Slurp some chicken soup. ☺

349. Attend the children's story hour at the library. ☺

350. Watch a holiday movie even if it isn't a holiday. ☺

351. Make a bonfire. ☺

352. Make a fresh flower arrangement
to brighten up your home or
to give to a friend. ☺

353. Think only nice thoughts. ☺

354. Write a short story about your
problems and have everything
end happily; then put it away
until the next time you are feeling blue. ☺

355. Teach your dog or other
      pet a new trick. ☺

356. Go white water rafting. ☺

357. Jump on a trampoline. ☺

358. Browse through an electronic store and play with all the gizmos. ☺

359. Mellow out. ☺

360. Rent a costume and wear it around town. ☺

361. Reach a compromise. ☺

362. Make a music video or comedy with your camcorder. ☺

363. Play in the ocean waves. ☺

364. For the rest of the day write
only with your left hand, or right hand
if you are normally a lefty. ☺

365. Watch old reruns of your
favorite football games. ☺

366. Brainstorm with a friend for ideas and solutions to your problems. ☺

367. Rearrange your furniture. ☺

368. Start a new family tradition, like family reunions at your house every leap year. ☺

369. Collect natural wood for sculptures. ☺

370. Read and reread the Bible. ☺

371. Buy a whirlpool maker for your
bathtub and use it. ☺

372. Bake bread. ☺

373. Attend a seance or conduct your own. ☺

374. Organize a scavenger hunt with friends. ☺

375. Make your own potpourris of dried flowers, herbs and spices. ☺

376. Give a loved one a big unexpected hug and kiss. ☺

377. Collect tree sap and make maple syrup. ☺

378. Learn a frivolous or outrageous skill such as lock picking, juggling, unicycling, or stilt walking. ☺

379. Bake a cake and a batch of cookies. ☺

380. Throw caution to the wind. ☺

381. Buy something subtle but elegant. ☺

382. Ride a double-decker bus. ☺

383. Secretly do a good deed
for someone. ☺

384. Kiss yourself all over. ☺

385. Flirt shamelessly. ☺

386. Strike a sexy pose in the mirror. ☺

387. Read a book you've been meaning to finish for a while. ☺

388. Ask a loved one for a big hug. ☺

389. Fill your house with sweet smelling pine branches and cones. ☺

390. Indulge a fetish. ☺

391. Go to the circus and sit in the front row with a bucket of popcorn and a souvenir pen light. ☺

392. Plant a peach pit. ☺

393. Drive a snowmobile. ☺

394. Treat yourself to the cutest stuffed animal you can find. ☺

395. Silk-screen holiday cards. ☺

396. Call a radio station and request your favorite song. ☺

397. Open all the windows and blinds in your house and let in the sunshine. ☺

398. Buy fancy lingerie. ☺

399. Put on your favorite outfit and jewelry and go out on the town. ☺

400. Play an old board game
from your childhood. ☺

401. Gently thump your thymus to
produce a calming sensation. ☺

402. Browse through a mall. ☺

403. Join a choir. ☺

404. Take flying lessons. ☺

405. Climb a tree and take in the view. ☺

406. Spend time with your family. ☺

407. Snowboard down the biggest hill. ☺

408. Enjoy a Rice Crispy treat. ☺

409. Practice smiling in the mirror. ☺

410. Do cartwheels in the grass. ☺

411. Serenade a loved one. ☺

412. Garnish a hat with dried flowers. ☺

413. Throw a formal dinner party. ☺

414. Choreograph your own hip-hop routine. ☺

415. Treat yourself to a manicure and a pedicure. ☺

416. Keep a journal of your favorite quotes. ☺

417. Take a foam toy in the tub with you. ☺

418. Make a wooden window box and plant all of your favorite flowers, seeds, and herbs. ☺

419. Take a friend out to lunch. ☺

420. Buy a one-of-a-kind item. ☺

421. Stick your head out the window of a moving car and breathe deeply. ☺

422. Ice skate at night on a frozen pond. ☺

423. Walk barefoot through the grass. ☺

424. Make soft sculpture caricatures of friends and family members. ☺

425. Enroll in a community college continuing education course. ☺

426. Browse through an antique shop. ☺

427. Sing in the shower. ☺

428. Write yourself a song. ☺

429. Go to the supermarket and stock up on your favorite foods. ☺

430. Indulge a fantasy. ☺

431. Believe in yourself. ☺

432. Visit the zoo with a child. ☺

433. Inhale the invigorating aroma
of newly cut grass. ☺

434. Give up your seat on the bus to an
elderly or handicapped person. ☺

435. Be spontaneous. ☺

436. Do a Toyota jump. ☺

437. Take an overnight train trip to an exotic locale. ☺

438. Read a trashy, steamy novel. ☺

439. Buy a new pen and write letters to your friends. ☺

440. Reward yourself. ☺

441. Play a simple game of catch
with your dog. ☺

442. Persevere in your dreams.
That's the only way they
can come true. ☺

443. Collect souvenirs from foreign places. ☺

444. Recall the funniest
moments of your life. ☺

445. Make your own opportunities. ☺

446. Take a two hour lunch break. ☺

447. Reread the best parts of your favorite books. ☺

448. Visit a hobby shop. ☺

449. Break off some pine needles and rub their scent on your hands. ☺

450. Prioritize your goals. ☺

451. Go on a shopping spree with a friend. ☺

452. Swim in a fountain. ☺

453. Record your problems and feelings in a diary. ☺

454. Take a walk through the newly fallen snow. ☺

455. Charter a boat and go
deep sea fishing. ☺

456. Try to break an outlandish
world record. ☺

457. Go to a fast food restaurant in a big overcoat with only pajamas on underneath. ☺

458. Take a museum tour. ☺

459. Make a wish box, memory box, and worry box and fill them accordingly. ☺

460. Baby-sit. ☺

461. Host a slumber party. ☺

462. Have a late night snowball fight. ☺

463. Make a tape and send it to a friend in lieu of a letter. ☺

464. Vacation at a local spa for the day. ☺

465. Jump into a big pile of dry leaves. ☺

466. Imagine your wishes coming true. ☺

467. Go down to the harbor and watch the boats sail off. ☺

468. Take a moonlight cruise. ☺

469. Revisit your college dorm, the
house your grew up in, and
your childhood playground. ☺

470. Go skiing and ride the ski lift
over and over. ☺

471. Wash your hair with fragrant shampoo. ☺

472. Vint your own wine. ☺

473. Visit a lighthouse and take in the ocean air and view. ☺

474. Take a leisurely walk through a scenic neighborhood and collect pine cones. ☺

475. Start a hobby shelf. ☺

476. Go window shopping at night on Fifth Avenue or Rodeo Drive. ☺

477. Play make believe. ☺

478. Attend an auction and bid a bit more than you really should. ☺

479. Quit worrying. ☺

480. Serve tea by the sea. ☺

481. Have a garage sale. ☺

482. Go to a matinee. ☺

483. Buy a basket and fill it with fruit and candy to give as a present. ☺

484. Listen to a radio talk show. ☺

485. Let your imagination run wild. ☺

486. Fill every niche of your house with sweet scented potpourri. ☺

487. Strip for your lover. ☺

488. Use paper plates so you don't have to do the dishes. ☺

489. Decorate your outdoor trees with strings of little white lights. ☺

490. Sit outside and listen to the wind chimes tinkle in the autumn wind. ☺

491. Cut out the clutter in your life. ☺

492. Give yourself a back scratch. ☺

493. Solve one of your problems or at least come to some decision in that regard. ☺

494. Chop wood even if you don't have a fireplace. ☺

495. Get an ancient recipe book and cook one of its exotic dishes. ☺

496. Practice your yoga or tai-chi in the shower, at the beach, or in the nude. ☺

497. Think peaceful thoughts while fly-fishing. ☺

● BLUES BUSTERS ●

498. Start saving for something you really want. ☺

499. Prune and shape a bonsai tree. ☺

500. Eat the most sinfully delicious and fattening dessert you can find. ☺

173

501. Browse through a vintage
clothing store. ☺

502. Accept that which you
cannot change. ☺

503. Sit and relax in your favorite chair. ☺

504. Finish something you started. ☺

505. Watch the late late movie. ☺

506. Clear your desk and start working. ☺

507. Splash around in a wading pool. ☺

508. Build an igloo. ☺

509. Start watching a cheesy
soap opera. ☺

510. Analyze why you are sad. ☺

511. Remind yourself that you matter. ☺

512. Lounge around and just pamper yourself with lotions, creams, powders, and fragrant soaps. ☺

513. Watch the sun rise. ☺

514. Go to sleep hugging a stuffed animal from your childhood. ☺

515. Do a load of wash and put on some crisp fresh clothes. ☺

516. Start your own home aquarium. ☺

517. Run warm water over your feet and wrists. ☺

518. Dance cheek-to-cheek. ☺

519. Rent a red convertible, roll down the windows, and play the music loud. ☺

520. Go cross country skiing through the woods. ☺

521. Draw a chalk picture on the sidewalk in the middle of town. ☺

522. Build a dollhouse out of tiny logs and stones. ☺

523. Apply a herbal hot pad to your chest. ☺

524. Create something from your imagination (e.g. make a puppet). ☺

525. Take a vacation in a log cabin nestled in the quiet woods. ☺

526. Play water sports. ☺

527. Check into a fancy hotel for the weekend and order room service. ☺

528. Put fresh clean sheets and blankets on your bed. ☺

529. Sleep in your guest room or den. ☺

530. Have a heart to heart talk with
a loved one. ☺

531. Listen to the patter of rain on the
windowpane. ☺

532. Pick wild flowers. ☺

533. Laugh out loud. ☺

534. Get actively involved in a social
cause you've felt strongly
about for years. ☺

535. Borrow someone else's clothes
and wear them. ☺

536. Take pictures of your surroundings
to serve as mementos
in the future. ☺

537. Treat yourself to new and festive socks and underwear. ☺

538. Finger paint on big sheets of paper and then use your creation for wrapping or wall paper. ☺

539. Organize a swap meet with friends. ☺

540. Vacation at a dude ranch. ☺

541. Host a costume, dinner, or cocktail party with a specific theme like a backwards party - everything from invitations to clothes must be backwards. ☺

542. Ride your bike to work
and all around town. ☺

543. Put together a tape of your
favorite music mix. ☺

544. Get a sunless tan. ☺

545. Have a picnic in a sailboat. ☺

546. Take a short single engine airplane ride over your home town. ☺

547. Make a wreath of dried backyard flowers. ☺

548. Find the smoothest rock, paint it, and use it as a paperweight. ☺

549. Start a dream diary. ☺

550. Vacation at a nudist colony. ☺

551. Build yourself a window seat. ☺

552. Visit an observatory. ☺

553. Buy a beauty magazine and follow one of its beauty tips. ☺

554. Buy some fresh fruits and vegetables at a farmer's market. ☺

555. Turn off your alarm and sleep late. ☺

556. Plan an African safari. ☺

557. Tickle your lover. ☺

558. Eat Japanese style. ☺

559. Ask for advice. ☺

560. Practice signing your name more artistically. ☺

561. Buy the daily newspaper and leisurely read it in the park. ☺

562. Give your significant other a sponge bath. ☺

563. Sleep under the stars in a sailboat. ☺

564. Consult an Ouji Board. ☺

565. Write one thing on today's
To Do list: Nothing. ☺

566. Watch a Walt Disney animated classic you enjoyed as a child. ☺

567. Organize your day with only your happiness in mind. ☺

568. Lend a sympathetic ear to someone else who is also blue. ☺

569. Randomly pick a blues buster and do it. ☺

About the Authors:

Jessica Is an undergraduate at Cornell and Michele is a law
student at Yale Law School. Both still experience a bit of the
blues every now and then while trying to finish their many papers
required for graduation. Out of their school related anxieties
and procrastination sprang many of their ideas for Blues Busters.